7/7

Published by Creative Educational Society, Inc., 123 South Broad Street, Mankato, Minnesota 56001. Copyright © 1977 by Creative Educational Society, Inc. International copyrights reserved in all countries. No part of this book may be reproduced in any form without written permission from the publisher. Printed in the United States.
Library of Congress Cataloging in Publication Data
Paige, David.
Robert Redford.
SUMMARY: A biography of the popular actor who starred in the films, "Butch Cassidy and the Sundance Kid," "The Sting," and "All the President's Men."
1. Redford, Robert—Juvenile literature. 2. Moving-picture actors and actresses—United States—Biography—Juvenile literature. [1. Redford, Robert. 2. Motion picture actors and actresses] I. Title.
PN2287.R283P3   791.43'028'0924 [B]   [92]   76-40604   ISBN 0-87191-554-5

ROBERT REDFORD

WRITTEN BY
DAVID PAIGE

DESIGNED BY
GENE KOHLER

CREATIVE EDUCATION
CHILDRENS PRESS

Since movies and movie stars were first projected on the screen, men have eyed the dazzling beauties who have appeared there. Marilyn Monroe, Elizabeth Taylor, Sophia Loren, and Raquel Welch are only a few of the many.

The sport of falling for movie stars, however, has not been limited to the male sex. Even before the Equal Rights Amendment and women's lib, girls had very much laid claim to participating in their version of this sport, namely admiring male movie stars.

There have been, however, only a handful of men in the history of the movies who have possessed that certain electricity to make them an idol to millions of women in the United States. Not many have been able to cause a near-riot when they go out in public. You can count on both hands those rare ones who, when they walk by, stop a woman in her tracks and leave her gaping wide-eyed at them. There are only that special few who see women scream, or grab at their clothes, or even faint when they come face to face.

There were Rudolph Valentino, Clark Gable, Cary Grant, Frank Sinatra, Paul Newman, and Elvis Presley. There have been very few others in that league. Some of them are gone now; others have gotten older. Either way, they are no longer the "love-idols" they once were.

The women of the United States, however, are not without such a "hero" today. They have found just the person in the blond-haired, blue-eyed, extraordinarily handsome young man named Robert Redford. He has all the qualities and charm of the best of the movie "love-idols." A person once said about Robert Redford, "A girl approaches him as though he were an altar."

4

Needless to say, Robert Redford has enormous popularity today. He is in the class of the superstar. But he is not, by any means, just a handsome face, topping off a trim, athletic body. He isn't simply a dream or a love symbol to the girls and women of America. He is an exceptionally fine actor and an intelligent and uniquely individual human being as well.

Robert Redford puts up with the idolizing; it's part of the motion picture business. There's actually not much else he can do about it. He even laughs about it sometimes. Not too many years ago, however, he *never* suspected that he would be such an object to the women of America, much less a superstar of the highest rank.

Robert Redford was born in Santa Monica, California, on August 18, 1937, in the shadow of Hollywood, the movie capital of the world. The family, which consisted of his father, who was an accountant for a large oil company, his mother, and a half-brother who was slightly older than Robert, moved to the town of Van Nuys shortly after Robert's birth. It was here that Robert Redford spent most of his youth.

Robert Redford's early years were not out of the ordinary. He went to school and was an average student. He was, however, an excellent athlete who loved sports and the outdoors. Even during these young years, he was restless and did not like to be "settled-down" or a victim of routine. What he wanted to grow up to be, in fact, was a soldier of fortune.

One thing Robert Redford took up in those days — perhaps to get in condition for the adventurous life of a soldier of fortune — was "climbing." "My stepbrother . . . and I used to do some wild things as

kids, like climbing buildings around Hollywood. Once we climbed a big Socony Gas sign. . . . Then when we were about 12, mountains got to us. . . . When we talked about climbing to the other kids, they thought we were out of our minds. I'd like to say that I climb mountains because they're there, but that doesn't say enough. I love the feeling of freedom you get from it."

As a teen-ager, Robert Redford attended the public high school in Van Nuys. He played on the school's football and baseball teams and also pursued his hobby of mountain climbing.

Growing up in the 1950's was different from what it is today. That was the time of crew-cuts and duck-tail haircuts, white bucks and blue suede shoes, and pink shirts with very narrow black and pink ties. Girls wore pedal-pushers and dresses that hung well below the knee and they also wore bobby sox; pantyhose weren't even invented then.

The stars of the day, to teen-agers anyway, were such people as James Dean, Debbie Reynolds, Elvis Presley, Sal Mineo, Pat Boone, and Natalie Wood. It was a time that could be called almost silly in some ways — music, for example. Frankie Laine sang "Mule Train." Johnny Ray really cried as he sang "Cry." Pattie Paige had a smash hit with "Doggie in the Window." But then Bill Haley and the Comets got a new form of music off to a wild start with "Rock Around the Clock," and the age of rock n' roll was born.

Television, so much a part of life today, had *just* become very popular. The big shows of the day were "I Love Lucy," "Leave It to Beaver," "Mr. Peepers," and "The Jackie Gleason Show."

It was during these years that Robert Redford developed his first liking for the movies. He went often. Popular in those days were the "rugged" movies: *Rebel Without a Cause, Blackboard Jungle, On the Waterfront, From Here to Eternity, High Noon.* It was also the time of lavish musicals like *An American in Paris, Gigi, The King and I, Oklahoma.* In Hollywood, the big names included Marilyn Monroe, Humphrey Bogart, Kim Novak, Tony Curtis, and Elizabeth Taylor. As he watched the glamor and the drama of the movies, however, he had no plans then to become part of it, much less to be one of the brightest stars in it.

Robert Redford's opinion of those days — the 1950's — was not very high: "I grew up in a state of indescribable boredom. I had a terrible time."

After high school, Robert Redford was able to get away from California and the boredom he felt there. He was such a good baseball player that he won an athletic scholarship to the University of Colorado. The university, located in Boulder, a picturesque town surrounded by the Rocky Mountains, was ideal for a young man who loved the outdoors and mountain climbing.

The arts were among his favorite studies in college. In fact, he decided to major in art at the university. He was also an avid reader of many different kinds of books, especially contemporary authors like John Dos Passos, James T. Farrell, and Thomas Wolfe.

The restlessness, however, was still there. The routine and discipline of college was not his favorite approach to life. Because he still harbored the dreams of distant places, different people, exciting things to do, he decided to go to those places, meet those people, and do those things. He left college after a little more than one year.

8

While he had been going to school, he had worked several summers as a laborer for the same oil company that employed his father. As a result, he had saved some money, enough to get him to Europe. He withdrew it from the bank and left to explore that fascinating continent.

For the next year, he traveled there — Paris, Rome, Florence. . . . He wanted to see and live in the great centers of art in Europe. It was an exciting and interesting way to continue his art studies. While he was there, he sketched and painted as well; but he could not make a living from it.

It was not necessarily an easy way of life during the year that he was in Europe. He lived poorly, scrounging here and there for food and money to pay for a place to sleep. But it was freedom; and it was interesting, adventuresome, and abundant with new things and places and people. A year in Europe is a marvelous experience; Robert Redford made the most of it.

At the end of the year, however, he decided to return to the United States. He did not go back to California, though, nor did he return to the mountains of Colorado. Instead he went to New York City, whose mountains have windows and whose paths are paved with asphalt and glutted with cars, trucks, and people. It was very different from the "great outdoors" he had been so fond of.

Surprisingly, however, Robert Redford liked New York. He found a different kind of excitement there and a different kind of freedom. He also discovered a sense of competition, which was something he had liked since his early days as an athlete. New York was a challenge, a new and different one; but he was prepared to meet it.

Once again he took up the study of art and design, enrolling at the Pratt Institute in Brooklyn, a well-known school of engineering and applied arts. Robert Redford decided that he would make a career of commercial art, and set to work to establish the training and experience necessary to make a living in that field.

Two important things happened in his life during those New York years. First, he met a young girl from Utah named Lola Van Wegenen. She was very pretty and very intelligent. She also liked the outdoors, and she even liked mountain climbing. She also apparently liked Robert Redford as much as he apparently liked her. It did not take long, once they both realized that, for their relationship to become as serious as a relationship can. They were married in September, 1958, one month after Robert Redford had become 21 years old.

The second major thing that happened in his life about that time was in regard to his art education. He had decided to take a course or two at the American Academy of Dramatic Art in New York. The reason, however, had nothing to do with becoming an actor — at least at the start. It was actually an extension of his art studies; it was for the purpose of learning something about set design and stage scenery.

The result, not surprisingly, was that Robert Redford found that he liked acting very much. In fact, he was so taken with it as a profession and an art form that he made the decision to change the goal of his career from commercial art to acting. It was a big decision in his life, but it would prove to be a very wise one. Millions of girls and women throughout the United States, needless to say, are very happy he made that decision. They are no different, perhaps, than the millions of men and boys who are equally happy that, say, Ann-Margret chose show business instead of accounting.

The decision was really the beginning of a slow and rigorous process, the fundamental work of learning the intricate craft of acting. It involved hard work and long hours; it was hope and frustration. Success did not follow immediately. On the other hand, it was not terribly distant either.

Robert Redford had two things going for him: his great good-looks and a natural talent for the art of acting. He also had determination, and he was not afraid to face a challenge. Those qualities are not just the assets of a good actor, they are *requirements.*

A good actor should also have a strong sense of freedom. He cannot be inhibited in his actions. He must, of course, have a powerful drive to express himself, and he needs to observe others. As Robert Redford himself said, "It's attitudes you watch when you're with people in public situations — Greyhound Bus depots, Madison Square Garden during a Knicks game . . . where they're being themselves. . . ."

To express himself and observe the reactions of others, an actor often does downright crazy things. Marlon Brando spent more than a little time throwing water-filled balloons down on unsuspecting pedestrians who chanced to walk under his apartment window. There was hardly anything that James Dean would not do, no matter how strange; and the practical jokes of John Wayne are legendary in Hollywood.

Robert Redford was not inhibited either. In his early days in New

York, his antics were as wild as anyone's. He described a few of them in a recorded discussion he once had with Ralph Nader, the famous crusader for safety, quality, and honesty in the production of consumer goods.

Redford explained, "I like to do some pretty goofy things . . . I like to cut loose, stand on my hands. When I was going to drama school, I once walked from 73rd Street and Columbus to 52nd and Broadway in my pajamas, just to see what the reaction would be. Once I sat for an hour in a wire garbage can on 54th Street; just got all crouched down in there and watched people coming and going."

It would be safe to say that Robert Redford was not inhibited. There must have been, however, more than a few rather startled people who saw that then unknown face staring out at them from inside a garbage can. New York is home to many odd things and sees strange actions by some rather weird people. No doubt Robert Redford contributed just a little to the zaniness of that city in the years he lived there while he was studying to be an actor.

Redford's first break came in early 1959. He won a brief walk-on part in *Tall Story,* a play about a basketball player, which was being produced on Broadway. It was not much of a debut. In fact, hardly anyone even noticed him. Everyone has to start somewhere, though.

That was it, too, for the next 11 months. Then he was given another role in a play called *The Highest Tree.* Once again, it was a very small part; and again he went unnoticed.

The following year, 1960, however, he found a new road to explore for his acting talents. He decided to try his luck at landing parts in television dramas. At the time, most of these were being produced in

12

California, so the Redfords packed up and headed back to the area where Robert had grown up. Life in California now was not going to be nearly so dull as it had been when Redford was a boy.

Despite his new way of life, however, Robert Redford still did not like Hollywood. He did, however, earn some roles in major television shows, practically from the very beginning. They ranged from serious drama on the highly-praised show "Playhouse 90" to parts in serials like "Perry Mason."

The parts still were relatively small — at least they were not the starring roles —; but some important people in the world of show business were beginning to take notice of this young man with the extraordinary good looks.

Redford had all the attributes of a leading man: he was handsome, with natural blond hair; he photographed well; he was a shade under 170 pounds, a weight which he carried on a lean, athletic body that was an inch or two under six feet in height. In describing him, someone once said, "He looks the way everyone would like the boy next door to look."

Robert Redford was not interested in simply being another handsome face. He wanted to be an actor, and a good one at that. He was more concerned with the quality of his art than with the image of himself.

For the Redfords as the decade of the 1960's began, things were scant. Money from the television parts and small roles on the Broadway stage was far from plentiful; but Robert was working, and he was growing in his profession. A highlight in his personal life did occur that year, however. He and his wife welcomed their first child, a little girl they named Shauna.

As 1960 drew to a close, Robert Redford went back to New York to act in the play *Little Moon of Alban,* which starred Julie Harris, one of the finest and most respected actresses in the theater. It was a much larger role than any he had previously had on Broadway; but despite fine acting from both Julie Harris and Robert Redford, the play itself was a failure, and he was back on the street looking for work again.

Then things began to look up. During the next two years, the television offers increased considerably. The parts, too, were more important ones in many instances, and the shows were among the most popular then on television — "Alfred Hitchcock Theater," "The Untouchables," "Dr. Kildare," "Route 66," "Naked City."

There were, importantly, two other things during those two years which had an enormous impact on Robert Redford's career.

First, he made his debut in the movies. Those people behind the scenes in the motion picture business who had been watching the development of the handsome young actor thought that now was the time to move. Redford was given a supporting role in the movie *War Hunt,* which starred John Saxon. In the movie, he was to play a sensitive, young soldier in the Korean War who runs into conflict with another soldier (Saxon) who is obsessed with violence and essentially insane. The two soldiers are trying to help a Korean orphan boy, each in his own way. They finally meet in a showdown of sorts, and the sensitive soldier, played by Robert Redford, prevails. The other soldier is killed in the same violent way he lived. Both the movie and the acting of Robert Redford received high praise from

the movie critics. It was a very good beginning.

The other boost to his career was the offer of the *lead* role in a Broadway comedy, *Sunday in New York.* That play, too, was a success; and Robert Redford received good reviews for his performance.

1962 had been a good year for Robert Redford. He had made excellent headway in establishing himself as a good actor on the live Broadway stage and in television and motion pictures as well.

The year was also one of importance in his personal life. The Redford's had their second child, a boy this time. They named him Jamie.

The following year was, for all practical purposes, the last in which Robert Redford devoted much of his time to television. The other offers were too good and too many. That year, however, he did receive a nomination for an "Emmy," the highest award presented in the television industry, for a supporting role in the television play, "The Voice of Charlie Pont." He did not win the award; but it was the first major, public recognition of his acting talents.

In 1963 there was also a new comedy in the making for the Broadway stage, *Barefoot in the Park.* It was written by a then relatively unknown playwright named Neil Simon. Robert Redford earned the starring role in this play about a young couple and the problems they encounter adjusting to married life as they set up house in New York City's Greenwich Village.

The show opened in late autumn of 1963, and met with instant success. It was riotously funny, and it became the smash hit of the year on Broadway. Robert Redford and his co-star Elizabeth Ashley were also highly praised for their performances.

Neil Simon went on to become Broadway's foremost writer of comedy and certainly one of the most successful playwrights in the history of American theater. *Barefoot in the Park* has become a standard which has been seen and enjoyed on stage, in movie houses, and on home television sets by literally millions of people.

From that moment on, Robert Redford's career as an actor was firmly established. People were not yet stopping him in the streets or rushing to his table in a restaurant to hound him for autographs; but the important people in the entertainment business knew him, and they recognized that his star was definitely on the rise.

Robert Redford appeared in *Barefoot in the Park* for almost a year. Playing the same role night after night is a grueling thing for any actor or actress. It can last only so long. Then the performer must seek new shows, new parts, new audiences, new challenges. Robert Redford was certainly aware of this.

The new challenges for him were now in Hollywood. Motion pictures was the place to be, and it was not surprising that the offers to be in films were picking up noticeably now.

Robert Redford went into two films right away. One was a comedy that unfortunately was not very funny, *Situation Hopeless But Not Serious.* The other movie, *Inside Daisy Clover,* was much more serious. In it he starred with the popular and beautiful actress, Natalie Wood.

Neither film was very successful, nor were the two dramatic movies that he made the following year — *The Chase* with Marlon Brando and *This Property Is Condemned,* again with Natalie Wood as his co-star.

In these movies, Robert Redford showed that he was a versatile actor. He could handle light comedy as well as a variety of roles in serious drama.

It was a period in Robert Redford's life when he sat just on the other side of the fence from being what could truly be called a star. He had starring roles, no doubt about that, but he was still not what you would call a "star."

Robert Redford was getting restless again. He had met the challenges of motion pictures but had not yet found the self-satisfying success he strove for. In addition, he was spending too much of his time and his family's time in Hollywood and on movie sound stages. Once again he sought the freedom that he had always held in such high respect. To satisfy this, he took his family to Europe for an extended vacation. They stayed almost a year, visiting historic cities and experiencing the rural, mountainous countryside of Spain. When the year ended, it was time again to return and face the challenges of his career.

In Hollywood, it had been decided to make a movie of the play *Barefoot in the Park*. Robert Redford was a logical choice to repeat the role that he had played so well on the Broadway stage. He accepted the offer. Jane Fonda was asked to co-star, and she accepted, too. The movie was released in 1967. It was an enormous success both with the critics and in the cash registers at the box offices.

This was Robert Redford's sixth movie, the one that pushed him over the fence into the world of stardom. It established him as a star

who could not only satisfy the critics but also bring the people off the streets and into the movie theaters.

Two years, however, would pass before Robert Redford's now well-known face would appear in a new movie. It was not that he was not sought after by the movie studios. On the contrary, *Barefoot in the Park* had made him a very hot item. But Redford wanted to make sure that he got the "right" movie. He remembered that the first five movies were *not* successful. His sixth was. He was very good in it; it had been "right" for him. He did not want to get a reputation for being good in *un*successful movies. The way to avoid that was to make absolutely certain he took only the roles that were best suited to his talents.

In 1969 Robert Redford showed up in *three* different movies. *Tell Them Willie Boy Is Here,* a powerful drama, saw him cast as a sheriff, engaged in relentlessly tracking down a renegade Indian. In *Downhill Racer,* Redford played a skier who participates in all the great international races and finally ends up winning a gold medal at the Olympics. It is the story of the adventures, challenges, and loves he encounters both on and off skis. The part was ideal for Robert Redford because, ever since his days in Colorado, he was an excellent and dedicated skier. He fit into the role perfectly.

Neither of these two movies would be considered a "smash hit," on the other hand they were both well-received.

The third movie of 1969, however, was something altogether different. Robert Redford teamed with Paul Newman to star in *Butch Cassidy and the Sundance Kid.* On the screen, the combination was dynamite. Paul Newman played Butch Cassidy and Robert Redford was the Sundance Kid, the two, a pair of likeable, funny, and bumbling bank robbers.

The movie was a gigantic success. It grossed more than $44 million.

At the end of 1969, after *Butch Cassidy and the Sundance Kid,* Robert Redford was established as one of the top stars in Hollywood. Because of this, he was able to start his own motion picture production company, which he named Wildwood Productions.

Only the very top actors and actresses — such superstars as Bob Hope, John Wayne, Lucille Ball, Paul Newman or Marlon Brando can successfully launch and maintain their own production companies. They can do it because they are the tremendously famous. If they star in a motion picture, it has a very good chance of success at the box office. By having their own production companies, the actor or actress, who is after all responsible for the movie's success, gains a much bigger share of the profits. Robert Redford had now entered into that class of superstar.

In 1970, Robert Redford replaced horses and skis with a motorcycle. He starred as a "rotten-to-the-core" motorcycle racer in *Little Fauss and Big Halsy.* As Big Halsy, Robert Redford was a liar and a scoundrel of the worst kind. It certainly was not the typical Robert Redford image. In the movie, however, he proved that he could play the "rat" as well as the hero.

After his escapades on the motorcycle, Robert Redford again disappeared from the movie screen for two years. He had become very active in the fight to preserve our environment against the people and industries that were spoiling it. Robert Redford had

always loved the outdoors and nature. He saw it being destroyed by thoughtless people. Appalled at what he saw, he joined the fight to save it.

Robert Redford was interested in important issues. He felt strongly that there was much more to life than merely being a famous star or a good actor, but it was hard for him to get his message across. As he explained it himself, ". . . lots of times I get the impression that people don't care what I think about environmental issues, pollution, politics. They want to know [instead] if I really jumped off the cliff in *Butch Cassidy* . . ."

Serious causes, however, need people like Robert Redford to help bring their importance to the attention of all the people in the United States. He gave very freely of his time to the cause, and still does.

In 1972, he was back before the eyes of the moviegoers of America. Once again, after a two-year vacation, he appeared in three separate movies during the first year of his return. Among them was *The Candidate* in which he played a young man running for the United States Senate who, as the campaign progresses, becomes less and less idealistic and more and more a cold-blooded, even corrupt politician.

Robert Redford enjoyed making *The Candidate*. Like his interest in other important issues, politics were of deep concern to him. He campaigned strongly for honesty in politics. In addition, he pushed for issues that were important to *all* the people, and he took sides politically for those candidates who pursued these issues.

Once again, he was not sure just how much his *presence* would help. In regard to his going to a rally for a political candidate, he

24

said, "People may show up, that's true; but I think it's a mistake to think that 2,000 curiosity-seekers represent 2,000 votes. They just want to see whether I'm fatter or shorter or balder or skinnier than I am on the screen." There's probably a little truth and a little error to that statement.

In his next movie, *Jeremiah Johnson,* Redford took on a completely different kind of role. As a strong-willed and bearded mountain man, he fought against wolves, Indians, the snows, and the rugged nature of the wilderness itself. His wife and the child who was entrusted to him were murdered by warlike Indians. He set out to avenge their deaths. It was indeed a difficult role, but Robert Redford played it convincingly. The critics found his performance "stirring," "true-to-life," "powerful." Along with the Sundance Kid, it was perhaps his finest bit of movie acting so far.

Although he was no Jeremiah Johnson, Robert Redford was, and is, a mountain man in his own way. With mountain climbing, skiing, and a home for himself and his family in the mountains of Utah he certainly qualifies for that title.

The third motion picture that year was a "semi-comedy," *The Hot Rock.* In it, he plays a thief who steals a fabulous diamond, first from a museum, then from a police station, and finally from a safety deposit box in a bank. The movie is funny in parts, serious in other places. It was, however, one of the least successful of Robert Redford's movies. Even the critics were not pleased with his performance.

Then there was 1973.

Barbra Streisand, famous as a singer, was selected to play her

first dramatic role in a movie. It was a love story called *The Way We Were*. Opposite her was the screen's most popular "idol" of the day, Robert Redford. The combination of Redford and Streisand was dazzling. There was good music, — the title song won the Academy Award that year — and there was laughter and sadness. The movie was an all-around smashing success.

It was not so much a hit, however, as the other movie Robert Redford starred in that year. Teamed once again with Paul Newman, the two brightened motion picture screens throughout the country with *The Sting*. The movie was the story of two likeable con-men — not greatly different in style from the bank robbers in *Butch Cassidy and the Sundance Kid*. The two took on the ultimate challenge, to con, or "sting," a big-time Chicago gangster out of a million dollars. They mapped out their dangerous game down to the very last detail, and pulled off the "sting" with one of the wildest surprise endings in the history of motion pictures.

Both Newman and Redford were as good in *The Sting* as they had been in *Butch Cassidy.* . . . Often, when two stars as famous as these two are cast alongside each other in equally important roles, the result is disaster. Each often tries to out-act the other. This has never been the case, however, with Paul Newman and Robert Redford. They actually complement each other, and each adds a certain extra quality to the performance of the other instead of detracting from it.

For his performance, Robert Redford was nominated for an Academy Award, the Oscar for *best actor*.

As a result of the splendid acting, the magnificent Scott Joplin music which had been adapted by Marvin Hamlisch, the fine plot, and the authentic setting, *The Sting* was the movie of the year. It became one of the highest box office successes in history. By the time all the money is counted, it will probably have grossed more than $100 million.

When the Academy Awards were presented, *The Sting* won seven

Oscars, including the one for best picture of the year. The award for best actor, however, went to Jack Lemmon for his performance in *Save The Tiger.* It was a disappointment for Robert Redford, of course; but it had been a high honor just to be nominated.

The following year, Redford accepted the part of Jay Gatsby, an enormously wealthy bootlegger in the 1920's who falls in love with another man's wife and later dies tragically. The story was from the pen of one of America's finest novelists, F. Scott Fitzgerald. *The Great Gatsby,* which had been written in the 1920's, had been made into a movie once before. The new version was to have two top superstars, Robert Redford and Mia Farrow. Nothing was to be spared in making this lavish movie. *Millions* of dollars were to be spent on it. Everything possible was to be done to advertise and promote it. But somehow, despite all this, Hollywood could not sell the movie. It opened to dreadful reviews from the critics. People stayed away from the theaters. The movie was an incredible failure; and instead of earning millions of dollars, it lost millions.

The image of Robert Redford, however, did not sink with the disastrous movie about Jay Gatsby. Redford remained the "love idol" of America's girls and women. They still sighed when they looked at him. There was still that glow in their eyes.

He shrugged off the failure and thrust himself fully into his next movie, *The Great Waldo Pepper.* In it, he is a barnstorming pilot of the 1920's. It was an ideal part for him, and the critics praised his performance. *The Great Waldo Pepper* turned out to be much greater than *The Great Gatsby.*

After that came *Three Days of the Condor,* released at the end of

1975. Robert Redford was "Condor," the code name for a CIA agent, involved in some undercover intrigue. Starring with him were top performers Faye Dunaway and Cliff Robertson. The movie, however, came out at a time when the CIA was under great criticism for many of its secret and illegal operations. Even with its fine cast, the movie unfortunately received almost as severe criticism as the real-life CIA.

Politics again entered the scene in 1976. Robert Redford, through his company Wildwood Productions, had bought the motion picture rights to the book *All the President's Men*. It is the story of the Watergate crime, cover-up, and conspiracy as told by the two Washington Post reporters, Carl Bernstein and Bob Woodward, who discovered, investigated, and revealed it. It is the story of political crimes and of the tragic fall of the President of the United States, Richard Nixon, because of his involvement in the crimes.

All the President's Men is a major motion picture. At the same time, it is only another step in the ongoing career of one of the most popular actors in America.

The story of Robert Redford is nowhere near an ending. The reason, of course, is that the Robert Redford bandwagon continues to roll. There are new challenges to face, new performances to be made. Girls continue to swoon; critics keep on applauding. There is much for him still to do in his personal fight to save the environment, to maintain honesty in politics, and to strive to keep his art of acting pure and free.

He is working at it all, and that is why his story is a long way from completion.